Oct '05
Sally,
Bon appetit!
Love,
Cris

By Cris Evatt

SIMPLIFYING & ORGANIZING
How to Organize Your Closet...and Your Life!
How to Pack Your Suitcase...and Other Travel Tips
Simply Organized!
30 Days to a Simpler Life

RELATIONSHIPS
Opposite Sides of the Bed
The Givers & the Takers
Café Conversations on Love & Relationships
Stop Arguing with Reality

Intuitive Cuisine

Cooking
without
Measurements

Cris Evatt

Egghead Books
Princeville, Hawaii

Egghead Books
P. O. Box 223157
PRINCEVILLE, HI 96722
simplify@aloha.net

ISBN 0-9708181-5-7

Cooking/Vegetarian

First Egghead Books Edition: 2004

Printed in the United States of America
by Morris Publishing
3212 East Highway 30 • Kearney, NE 68847
1-800-650-7888

10 9 8 7 6 5 4 3 2 1

To Dave
for his garden, fruit trees,
chickens, and love

Pinches & Handfuls

If my editor would allow,
my recipes would say
"a handful of this"
and "a bit of that."
Not "two small onions,"
but "some onions."
And add lemon, if you have it.
Take as many potatoes,
as you think you want.
When parsley is plentiful,
use plenty.

—HELEN NEARING
Simple Food for the Good Life

Contents

Introduction

Great chefs rarely rely on measurements. Instead, they use rigid recipes as guidelines and starting points. Recipes are viewed as other people's improvisations and bright ideas. Professionals skim recipes and trust their intuition, experience, and tastebuds. They create anew.

I wrote this book because I wanted to become more innovative, like a professional chef, and not such a slavish devotee to recipes. I vowed to read recipes in a looser way, ignoring precise measurements—cups, teaspoons, tablespoons, ounces, and pounds. If I ignore the numbers, I thought, I'll feel liberated. Cooking will become an arena for being highly creative, flamboyant.

When I decided to become an Intuitive Cook, I owned fifty cookbooks which I rarely used. My approach to recipes had made me feel intimidated, sluggish. Consequently, my repertoire in the kitchen was stale and lacked originality.

Typically, our evening meals consisted of green salads topped with spiral pasta or roasted vegetables, fried rice and veggies, tacos or enchiladas, and Dave's special Portabella Gardenburgers with fresh herbs, lettuce, and avocado slices.

A few years ago, I noticed that a typical recipe is like a picture-puzzle waiting to be solved. Each recipe has three types of pieces: the basics, optional additions, and variations. And it's up to me to figure out which ingredients fall into these categories.

Oftentimes I wondered, *Why doesn't one cookbook omit measurements and just list ingredients?* I never discovered why. Perhaps you know the answer to this brazen, iconoclastic question.

Since I couldn't find a cookbook without precise measurements, anywhere, I decided to write this one. Teaspoons became pinches and dashes, and cups become dollops, heaps, and handfuls. And I became more playful in the kitchen.

— *Cris Evatt*

-1-

What's Intuitive Cuisine?

*A café on the shores of Lake Reality
in Kinnelon, New Jersey.*

*Preparing good food requires both intuition
and rational thought. The five senses—sight, smell,
taste, touch, and hearing—all contribute
to the process.*

—LYNN WALTERS
Cooking at the Natural Café in Santa Fe

Food is a poem. It speaks to us in eye-appealing colors, nose-tingling aromas, and mouth-watering tastes. When food is picked on the day it is eaten, it speaks even louder. Garden fresh lettuce, green beans, and tomatoes have more to say than produce trucked in from Salinas.

Ten years ago, I coined the term "Intuitive Cuisine" because I wanted to become more carefree in the kitchen. I wanted to stop feeling like a slave to my safe, stale routine.

What follows are *three realizations* that helped me become a less programmed, more experimental cook. These realizations gave me permission to do my own thing in the kitchen. Nowadays, I use recipes in cookbooks as guides—not gospels. I rely less on measurements and more on my intuition.

REALIZATION #1
Our two Inner Chefs
compete with one another.

We have two inner chefs lurking in our mind and seeking our undivided attention. First, there's our Intuitive Chef who supports our creative imagination. Then there's our Ego Chef who sabotages our attempts to improvise.

Intuitive Chef: A soothing inner voice who coaxes us to experiment with food. "Don't follow recipes verbatim," it says. "Use them as guides." My friend Robin calls her Intuitive Chef, Gramma Tucker, in honor of her grandmother, a free spirit in the kitchen.

Ego Chef: This petty, fearful chef says, "Don't veer from recipes. Be precise." Its strident voice puts you down, wants you to feel unworthy in the kitchen. It tells lies like, "Your Intuitive Chef is a charlatan, a lousy cook. Ignore it. I'm superior. Give me the power."

The Ego Chef is persistent, tries to sabotage your relationship with your Intuitive Chef. When it interrupts, tell it to "Get a job at McDonald's."

REALIZATION #2
Substitutions enlarge your repertoire.

Think *substitutes* as you read cookbook recipes. "What other vegetable will work in this recipe?" Don't become locked into the author's choices. Recipes are starting points, not destinations. And don't be impressed by glitzy cookbook covers with chefs in million-dollar kitchens.

Here are some common substitutions to use when restyling recipes. When they say:

•**Broccoli:** Think "Vegetables." Substitute okra, beets, carrots, cauliflower, leeks, potatoes, squash, kale, chard, and eggplant.

•**Sugar:** Think "Sweeteners." Sugar can mean honey, maple syrup, fruit sweeteners, brown rice syrup, and the herb *stevia*.

•**Pepper:** Think "Hot Stuff." Pepper can mean cayenne, fresh peppers, New Mexico hot sauces, Indonesian hot sauces (sambal oleck), and fresh ground peppers, like Lampong and Tellicherry.

Of course, following recipes verbatim is comfortable and substituting ingredients can feel rebellious. But why not rebel? What's the worst thing that can happen? Hisses, boos, catcalls, fake kudos?

REALIZATION #3
Recipes turn out different every time. Embrace the inconsistencies.

Recipes seldom turn out the same, even if we strictly follow directions. Spices and herbs age, fresh produce isn't always fresh, and our tastebuds give fickle readings. Again, great chefs seldom follow recipes. So why do we? Tradition? Insecurity?

The recipes in this book were not formally tested because each time they are cooked, they turn out different. Your results will only loosely emulate mine. So relax and have fun. Enjoy the process.

Add a pinch of this and a dollop of that. Add a little and taste a lot. Is there enough garlic? Should it be spicier? Will honey take the edge off? What will happen if dark chocolate is added?

-2-

French Bistro Formulas

Touring the LaVarenne Cooking
School in Burgundy with a French friend.

Bistro fare is not afraid to be lusty
and earthy…It is food without pretension.

—PATRICIA WELLS
Bistro Cooking

French goat cheese slathered on freshly-baked baguettes makes me swoon. So does reading in cozy cafés with a cup of *chocolat chaud*, a decadently thick and rich cup of hot chocolate.

I call myself a Hedonistic Vegetarian. Hedonists are unabashed pleasure-seekers who believe things like, "We're not here for a long time, we're here for a good time." And, "These are the good old days." Indeed life is too short to be self-denying.

France is teeming with people who are devoted to to enjoying themselves. While the French linger over two-hour lunches, we often eat on the run.

Recently, we swapped our house for an apartment in Paris where one of my missions was to discover why French women stay so thin and wear fewer overblouses. The Answer: They eat slower and are happier with smaller portions. A tiny apple fruit tart is enough. For us, it's a bite.

Simple Green Salad

FORMULA
salad greens
vegetables
fresh herbs
a vinaigrette (*see page 24)*

Wash the greens. Spin them dry on slow speed. Fast spinning presses the delicate leaves against the walls of the dryer. The fun begins when you invent your own salad.

VARIATIONS

Classic Niçoise Salad
On a bed on lettuce, place green beans, potatoes,
hard-boiled egg wedges, niçoise olives
(or other brine-cured black olives), red bell pepper
slices (optional), and tomatoes. If you occasionally
eat fish, add anchovies and canned tuna.

Colette's Salad
Almost everyday, Colette consumes a green salad.
"Eighty-percent of my diet is raw," she says.
Her favorite salad is made of mesclun lettuce,
some kale or chard leaves, grated beats and carrots,
celery slices, artichokes hearts, fresh basil and
parsley leaves, and a simple vinaigrette.

Create *3* Variations

"   "
_____

_____

_____

_____

"   "
_____

_____

_____

_____

"   "
_____

_____

_____

_____

_____

Designer Vinaigrettes

FORMULA
olive oil
wine vinegar
salt
pepper

ADDITIONS
garlic, *a hint*
mustard
shallots, *or other onions*
herbs & spices
sweetener

Design your own vinaigrettes. The ratio of vinegar to olive oil is about 4 to 1. Too much vinegar can ruin the dressing. Add olive oil last. Whisk it in slowly.

VARIATIONS

Honey-Mustard Vinaigrette
Add honey and Dijon mustard to the formula above.
For Papaya Seed Dressing: Add some papaya,
its seeds, and basil and/or oregano to taste.

Tarragon Vinaigrette
Use apple cider vinegar, any vegetable oil, mild onions,
tarragon, parsley, water, sugar, and salt. No pepper.

Create *3* Variations

"   "
_____

_____

_____

_____

"   "
_____

_____

_____

_____

"   "
_____

_____

_____

_____

_____

Soothing Puréed Soups

FORMULA
vegetable
onion
broth/water
potatoes, *optional (adds body)*
garlic, *optional*
herbs & spices
white pepper, *freshly ground*
salt, *or Bragg's*

Cover the ingredients with water. Bring them to a boil. Simmer the soup until the veggies are done. Let the soup cool, then purée it in batches. Reheat. Garnish with parsley, cilantro, chives, or green onions.

VARIATIONS

Winter Squash Soup
Add a chopped apple, grated ginger, and a pinch of cinnamon or nutmeg.

Edith Piaf's Carrot Soup
Season with chervil and fresh orange juice. Include some potatoes. You'll sing about it.

Broccoli Soup
Add a bunch of broccoli, a peeled and chopped pear and a dash of cayenne.

Create *3* Fillings

"_____"
_____

_____
_____
_____

"_____"
_____

_____
_____
_____

"_____"
_____

_____
_____
_____
_____

Garden Veggie Soups

FORMULA
vegetables, *beaucoup*
onions
water/broth
salt & pepper
herbs & spices, *optional*

ADDITIONS
tomatoes
potatoes
beans
pasta

Cover some vegetables with water. Bring them to a boil, then simmer. Partially-cook the denser vegetables, then add the faster-cookers. Mushy vegetables are passé.

VARIATION

Simone's Soup
Boil a mix of vegetables, sliced and
diced. When the veggies are done, add a pat
of butter, salt, and cayenne. C'est tout.

Bernard-Henri's Secret Stock
Carmelize some yellow onions and lots of garlic,
finely chopped. Start with water to cover,
then simmer. Add more water to make the stock.

Create *3* Variations

"   "
_____

_____
_____
_____

"   "
_____

_____
_____
_____

"   "
_____

_____
_____
_____
_____

Classic Quiches

FORMULA
piecrust, *buy or make*
eggs, *lightly beaten (3 large)*
salt & pepper
milk (*about twice as much as eggs*)
cheese, *grated*
vegetables, *chopped*

A quiche is a savory custard in a piecrust. Gently beat the eggs with salt and pepper. Add some milk. Place grated cheese on the bottom of the crust. Sauté the vegetables until the liquid evaporates. Watery vegetables don't work as well. A Pyrex pie dish can be used for baking. To tell when the quiche is done, gently move the dish to see if the top ripples. Go for a no-ripple-effect.

FILLINGS

Spinach Quiche
Steam handfuls of spinach. Drain well.
Add a sprinkle of freshly grated nutmeg.

Wild Mushroom Quiche
Soak dried mushrooms until they are soft.
Drain them and chop them. Sauté them in oil
and butter. Add them to the quiche.

Create *3* Variations

"   "
_____

_____
_____
_____

"   "
_____

_____
_____
_____

"   "
_____

_____
_____
_____
_____

The Intuitive Cook's
French Twists

• **What's a *mirepoix*?** To make a mirepoix, braise a mixture of finely chopped onions, celery, and carrots. This combo is often the first step in many soups, sauces, and stew recipes.

• ***Panade*:** Any kind of soup poured over day-old bread, thinly-sliced and rubbed with garlic. French onion soup is a "Panade a l'Oignon." A wide-mouthed earthenware dish is perfect for this soup.

• ***Soupe au Pistou*:** Soup with pesto stirred in at the end. Often a minestrone-style soup.

• **Niçoise Olives:** Niçoise means "as prepared in Nice," the French Riviera city. Niçoise olives are petite, oval olives grown in the Provence region.

• **Chévre:** A tart cheese made with pure white goat's milk. Look for the words "pur chévre" on the label...or cow's milk might be lurking inside. Goat cheeses range in texture from dry and firm to moist and creamy. They come in discs, cones, cylinders, and pyramid shapes.

• **Madeleines:** Petite spongy cakes resembling a scallop shell, baked in a special pan. Best eaten fresh from the oven. Dip madeleines into *thé or café*, tea or coffee.

• **Dijon for Burns:** When you receive a burn, reach for Dijon or French's mustard. Spread it liberally on the spot. Let it set for a few minutes. Voila! No pain.

-3-

East Indian

Formulas

Prem shows me how to make a chapati.

*If you can put one spice in a pan, you can just
as easily put ten or even fifteen. They all cook quickly.*

—MADHUR JAFFREY
Indian Cookery

A steamy chai is one of life's special treats. I love its spicy sweetness. In bookstore cafés, I sip chai while I'm reading magazines or a novel. In my home office, I drink it to perk me up, to help me focus when I'm on a writing binge.

In the eighties, I took Indian cooking lessons in Fiji from Prem Deo, an extraordinary cook whose parents were from Bijar, India. (*Prem* means "love.") Dave and I sailed there on our 43-foot sloop. The trip began in Sausalito, California, and took three years. We stopped at anchorages in Mexico, the Marquesas, Tuamotus, Tahiti, Tonga, and the Cook Islands before arriving in Fiji, our final destination.

One of my best friends, Nutan Brownstein, hails from Bombay. "Can you come for chai?" she often asks. When I come for lunch, I learn even more about Indian cookery. She reminds me of Prem.

Prem's Simple Chai

FORMULA
cloves, *crushed*
cardamom, *bruised*
cinnamon stick, *crushed*
nutmeg, *grated*
milk
water
black tea leaves

ADDITIONS
gingerroot, *freshly grated*
allspice
black peppercorns, *crushed*

First, Prem adds the four spices to a pan. Second, she adds milk and water, about one part milk to four parts water. She brings these ingredients to a boil, then adds loose tea leaves and lets them steep. Next she strains the chai with a fine mesh strainer. She asks her guests to sweeten their chai with brown sugar.

VARIATION

Nutan's Chai
Nutan uses a chai masala (mix of ground spices),
a few bruised cardamom pods, grated ginger,
organic milk, and black Indian tea leaves.
She cooks her brew in a stainless steel pan.

Create *3* Variations

"   "

_____

_____

_____

_____

"   "

_____

_____

_____

"   "

_____

_____

_____

_____

Prem's Basic Curries

FORMULA

Three Seeds: **cumin, mustard, fenugreek**
onions, *chopped*
garlic, *minced*
oil or ghee
vegetable(s)
Madras Masala (*a popular curry powder)*
turmeric *(use half as much as masala)*
fresh chilies or cayenne
salt
water
tomatoes (*may be added to any curry)*
fresh cilantro

- Heat a little oil or *ghee* (clarified butter in a jar that doesn't brown and keeps a long time). Fry the three seeds in hot oil. Be careful not to burn the fenugreek or it tastes bitter. Use less fenugreek than the other seeds. Mustard seeds pop—a good sign!
- Add chopped onions. Cook until translucent.
- Stir in the chopped garlic. Cook a few seconds.
- Add veggies, the masala, turmeric, chilies, salt and a splash water. Cover, simmer. Add water as needed.

VARIATIONS
Potato, Pea & Carrot Curry
Spinach/Kale/Chard Curry (*no turmeric*)
Eggplant Curry (*no turmeric*)

Create *3* Variations

"   "
_____

_____

_____

_____

"   "
_____

_____

_____

_____

"   "
_____

_____

_____

_____

_____

Indian-Style Enchiladas

FORMULA
whole-wheat tortillas
red enchilada sauce
veggie fillings *(see below)*
plain yogurt, *a dollop*
tamarind chutney, *or any chutney*

Make Indian enchiladas like you do Mexican ones. First, add some sauce to the bottom of a rectangular baking dish. Next, add a filling to the tortilla, roll up, and place in the dish, like a row of logs. Pour the sauce over the enchiladas. After they are hot and bubbly, let them set for a few minutes. Serve each enchilada with a dollop of yogurt and tamarind chutney.

FILLINGS

Sweet Potato Filling
Mash some sweet potatoes/yams. Add *garam masala,* a popular Indian spice mix. Add some chopped fruit such as bananas, raisins and pineapple. Experiment. Carrots and parsnips may be added, too.

Green Enchiladas
Cook a pot of greens (one or more kinds) and onions. Green beans can be added, too. Drain well. Add a little garam masala. Put the greens in a food processor and finely chop them. Don't purée them.

Create 3 Variations

"   "
_____

_____

_____

_____

"   "
_____

_____

_____

_____

"   "
_____

_____

_____

_____

_____

Spicy Potatoes

FORMULA
potatoes
onions & garlic
cumin seeds
cumin powder
garam masala
lemon juice, *optional*
cayenne/ peppers
salt
fresh cilantro leaves

In a skillet, fry the cumin seeds in a little oil. Add the onions and cook until translucent. Add garlic. Combine the potatoes with the seeds. Add garam masala, cumin powder, pepper, and salt. Sauté.

VARIATIONS

Green Beans & Coconut Spicy Potatoes
Add cooked green beans, mushrooms,
and lite coconut milk.

Green Spicy Potatoes
Steam a huge pot greens. Drain well. Combine.

Spicy Potato Samosas
Mash the potatoes and add peas. Place a scoop
in a whole wheat tortilla. Wrap. Cook both
sides on a lightly-oiled griddle.

Create *3* Variations

"   "
_____

_____
_____
_____

"   "
_____

_____
_____
_____

"   "
_____

_____
_____
_____
_____

Hearty Dal Soups

FORMULA

dals/split peas/lentils
turmeric, *a dash*
vegetables (*see variations below*)
salt, *to taste*
Three Seeds: **cumin, mustard, fenugreek**
oil or ghee
onions & garlic
gingerroot, *grated or minced*
tomatoes, *optional*
curry leaves, *optional*
fresh cilantro leaves
lemon/lime wedges

- Wash the dals. Soak them for about an hour. Add about 6 parts water to 1 part beans. Add a pinch of turmeric. Bring to a boil and remove the froth.
- Add the vegetable(s) after the beans are almost done.
- In a skillet, heat a little oil. Fry the seeds, then the onions and garlic. (Never add curry powder.)
- When the beans are done, add them to the skillet with the fried seasonings.

VARIATIONS

Eggplant Dal
Carrot, Tomato & Potato Dal
Cauliflower Dal
Spinach Dal

Create 3 Variations

"   "
_____

_____

_____

_____

"   "
_____

_____

_____

_____

"   "
_____

_____

_____

_____

Tomato Chutney

FORMULA

oil or ghee
***Three Seeds:* cumin, mustard, fenugreek**
onions & garlic
tomatoes, *fresh or canned*
cilantro, *heaps*
gingerroot, *grated*
brown sugar
Madras Masala (*curry powder*)
turmeric (*half amount of masala*)
chili peppers, *or cayenne*
salt
water, *as needed*

- Follow the directions for Prem's Basic Curries, see page 38. Where it says *add vegetables*, add tomatoes, cilantro, gingerroot, and sugar (counteracts the acidity of tomatoes). Simmer for an hour or so.
- Make huge potfuls. Freeze small portions. At my Indian dinners, the favorite condiment, bar none, is Tomato Chutney.

VARIATION

Fast-Track Tomato Chutney
Add some Indian spices to a jar of red pasta sauce.
Use ingredients you have on hand. Improvise.

Create *3* Variations

"   "
_____

_____

_____

_____

"   "
_____

_____

_____

_____

"   "
_____

_____

_____

_____

_____

Cilantro-Mint Chutneys

FORMULA
cilantro leaves
mint leaves
lemon/lime juice
water (*a little may be needed*)
salt

ADDITIONS
green chilies, *seeded and minced*
scallions/onion
garlic
gingerroot, *peeled and minced*

Play with the cilantro/mint ratio. Blend the ingredients into a paste. Cilantro-Mint Chutney doesn't keep well, so make it as you need it. Try the formula with Jalapeno peppers.

VARIATIONS

Mint Chutney
Add mint (no cilantro), lemon, chilies, onion, gingerroot, and a little superfine sugar.

Coconut-Cilantro Chutney
Add unsweetened shredded coconut.

Yogurt Mint Chutney
Add yogurt to the basic formula.

Create *3* Variations

"   "
_____

_____

_____

_____

"   "
_____

_____

_____

_____

"   "
_____

_____

_____

_____

Cooling Raitas

FORMULA
plain yogurt
vegetable(s), *diced or grated*
herbs/spices, *cumin, cilantro, mint,*
dill, parsley, chervil, tarragon
salt
pepper/cayenne, *optional*

Raitas are a refreshing contrast to spicy curries. They are made with yogurt, any raw vegetable, and some seasonings. Mix the ingredients together in a bowl. Chill. Try these soothing Indian raitas:

VARIATIONS

Cucumber Raita
Combine a peeled, seeded, and grated cucumber with ground cumin and minced mint and/or cilantro. (Don't ruin it with a bitter cucumber.)

Tomato Raita
Add a diced tomato, diced cucumber, salt, cayenne, and roasted cumin seeds.

Fruit Raitas
- Add seedless grapes, banana slices, and walnuts.
  - Add banana slices, dried coconut, and a squeeze of lemon.

Create *3* Variations

"   "
_____

_____

_____

_____

"   "
_____

_____

_____

_____

"   "
_____

_____

_____

_____

_____

The Intuitive Cook's
East Indian Tips

• **Darjeeling Tea:** Sitting on the porch of a bungalow on a tea planation in Darjeeling, you can see the peaks of Everest as you sip a cup of this strong, full-bodied black tea, grown at 7,000 feet. *Taster's Choice:* Tazo Darjeeling Organic Black Tea.

• **What's in a curry powder?** A curry powder is a "masala" or mixture of two or more ground spices. *Madras masala* and *garam masala* are favorites. Prem says, "Don't cook curry powders in oil, just cook seeds. Ground spices only require gentle warmth to release their flavors."

• **Patak's Garlic Pickles:** A four-star condiment for Indian Curry dishes. Beware, it's addicting! I use it as a topping for rice, quinoa, and baked potatoes. I also buy Patak's Lime Pickles. Most health food stores carry Patak's excellent products.

• **Tamarind:** Indian date-like fruit used in beverages and chutneys. Comes from a 5-inch-long pod and has a sour-sweet pulp. Buy in concentrated form from East Indian grocery stores. Lemon juice is a substitute.

-4-

Asian Formulas

*With my busy lifestyle, I find that using
the wok is the perfect answer to today's
fast-paced demands.*

—KEN HOM
Quick Wok

After living in Fiji, we hopped a plane for Japan where we dined on multi-coursed dinners of bite-sized servings on tiny dishes. The dishes were as intriguing as the food. During the day, I consumed hearty bowls of noodles and adzuki bean pastries.

Each generation looked taller than the preceding ones. What was that all about, I wondered? In Kyoto, our final stop, I found a likely explanation. There were twenty-one McDonald's there. A diet of more meat, wheat, and dairy caused the growth spurts. American kids are taller (and wider), too.

For many years, I didn't make sushi because I thought I had to use sticky white rice, which reminded me of cheap, airy white-bread. When I learned that short-grain brown rice could be substituted, I became ecstatic. Now I frequently make vegetarian sushi rolls.

Japonica Black Rice Medley

FORMULA
Lundberg's Japonica Rice, *cooked*
red pepper, *diced*
corn kernels
scallions, *sliced*
cashews, *roasted*
sesame seeds, *toasted in a pan*
rice wine vinegar, *to taste*
soy sauce, *to taste*
oil, *a splash*

- Japonica rice is a unique blend of a medium-grained mahogany-colored rice and jet-black rice, both originating in Japan. It's available in most health food stores.
- Put everything in a bowl. Toss gently. This dish is red, green, and yellow against a background of black.

AWARD WINNER FOR THE
Best Dish to Take to a Potluck Dinner!

VARIATIONS

Tricolor Rice Dishes
Instead of the three vegetables above,
add three others. Try peas, yellow peppers,
and tiny cherry tomatoes. Keep the veggies small.

Tip: Don't substitute brown rice.

Create 3 Variations

"   "
_____

_____

_____

_____

"   "
_____

_____

_____

_____

"   "
_____

_____

_____

_____

_____

Sushi Rolls

FORMULA
Nori sheets
sushi mat
short-grain brown rice
veggies, *long thin pieces*
wasabi
soy sauce
pickled ginger *(condiment)*

- Cook short-grain brown rice until it's sticky.
- Place a Nori sheet on a sushi mat. Add a scoop of rice and spread it thickly over the nori. Leave an inch of empty space at the upper end.
- Pick up the lower end and roll snugly. *For Precise Instructions:* Go to a sushi bar and watch the pros. Just buy a veggie roll, bowl of miso soup, and green tea.
- Let the roll set a few minutes before cutting with a moist knife.
- Combine soy sauce and wasabi to taste. Yum!

VARIATIONS

Vegetable Rolls
Place carrots and avocado strips
in the center of the rice.

Cucumber Rolls
Add cucumber, seeded and sliced lengthwise
into long narrow strips.

Create *3* Variations

"   "
_____

_____

_____

_____

"   "
_____

_____

_____

_____

"   "
_____

_____

_____

_____

_____

Chinese Stir-fry Sauce

FORMULA
soy sauce
sugar, brown
water/broth
cornstarch

ADDITIONS
rice wine/dry sherry
sesame oil, *to taste*
oyster sauce
rice vinegar
ginger, *chopped*
garlic
chili paste

Add a little oil to a frying pan or wok. When it's hot, stir-fry one or more vegetables. Mix the sauce ingredients in a bowl and add to the wok.

VARIATIONS

Snow Pea Stir-fry
String and stir-fry the snow peas. Add some mung bean sprouts. Flavor with sugar and rice wine.

Broccoli Stir-fry
Cut the florets in half. Peel the stalks and cut on a diagonal. Steam the broccoli in a little water. Add soy sauce, rice wine, ginger, and sesame oil.

Create *3* Variations

"   "
_____

_____

_____

_____

"   "
_____

_____

_____

_____

"   "
_____

_____

_____

_____

Mu Shu Vegetables

FORMULA
vegetable medley
eggs, *scrambled*
Stir-fry sauce (*see page 60*)
tortilla wraps
Hoisin sauce
scallions, *long slivers*

- In a bowl, create a stir-fry sauce from the formula
  on page 60.
- Scramble the eggs and set aside.
- Stir-fry some vegetables for the filling.
- Spoon Hoisin sauce on a tortilla and add
  the stir-fry vegetable mixture.
- Top the filling with scallion slivers.
- Roll up the tortilla like a wrap. (Try spinach and
  garlic-flavored wraps.)

VARIATIONS

Crunchy Veggie Filling
Cut up a bunch of bok choy.
Separate the leaves and stalks. Slice the stalks
diagonally into small pieces. Cut the leaves into strips.
Slice a seeded red bell pepper and some mushrooms.
Add mung bean aprouts. Stir-fry until tender-crisp.
Pour in the stir-fry sauce and
cook for a minute more.

Create *3* Variations

"   "
_____

_____

_____

_____

"   "
_____

_____

_____

_____

"   "
_____

_____

_____

_____

_____

Thai Vegetable Stir-Fries

FORMULA
vegetables
oil
red curry paste
fish sauce *(it's salty)*
brown sugar
fresh mint, *chopped*

This quickie curry formula is cooked by Thai people after a hard day of working in the fields. Balance the flavors—hot, sweet, sour and salty.

Instructions: Heat a tinsy splash of oil in a wok or pan. Add a little red curry paste and fry for a couple of minutes. Add some veggies and stir-fry. Add a pinch of sugar and splash of fish sauce. Stir-fry for another minute. Garnish with fresh mint, if it's easy to get. Transfer the dish to a serving bowl. (Coconut milk can be added to any Thai curry.)

VARIATIONS

Verdant Stir-fry
For vegetables, add cabbage, green beans (cut small), and shiitake mushrooms. For more protein, add flavored or plain tofu cubes.

Tricolor Stir-fry
Add broccoli, red peppers, and tiny corn-on-the-cobs.

Create *3* Variations

"   "
_____

_____
_____
_____

"   "
_____

_____
_____
_____

"   "
_____

_____
_____
_____
_____

Phad Thai

FORMULA
rice noodles/soba noodles/vermicelli
eggs, *lightly beaten*
vegetables
tofu, *optional*

PAD THAI SAUCE
lemon/lime juice
fish sauce
catsup (*tomatoes may also be added*)
sugar
cayenne/crushed red pepper flakes

FINISHING TOUCHES
fresh bean sprouts, *rinsed*
scallions, *sliced*
peanuts, *crushed*
fresh mint or cilantro, *chopped*
lime wedges, *place around dish*

- *Thailand's most loved noodle dish.* Soak rice noodles in hot water, as directed on the package. Rinse noodles in cold water, drain, and set aside.
- Scramble the eggs; remove and set aside. Combine sauce ingredients in a bowl. Add a dash of oil and stir-fry your favorite vegetables and tofu. Add sauce, noodles, and egg to the vegetable mix. Toss well.
- Add bean sprouts. Toss. Garnish with peanuts, cilantro, scallions, and limes.

Create 3 Variations

"   "
_____

_____

_____

_____

"   "
_____

_____

_____

_____

"   "
_____

_____

_____

_____

_____

Thai Soft Spring Rolls

FORMULA

spring roll wrappers
rice noodles or soba noodles
lettuce
mint & basil, *fresh*
vegetables, *julienned or grated*

SWEET-SOUR DIPPING SAUCE
lemon/lime, water, sugar, fish sauce,
minced garlic, crushed chili flakes

- Soak the rice noodles in hot water until they have the texture you like. Drain, rinse in cool water. If the noodles get sticky, gently toss them under cold water.
- Line up the vegetables.
- Soak one wrapper at a time for about 30 seconds in warm water. Then place the noodles and veggies in a horizontal row in the middle of the wrapper.
- *To Roll:* Start with the bottom edge. Roll up over the filling, pressing the ingredients into a cylinder shape. Bend the sides inward. Roll more. Create a tight little package. Serve the rolls whole or cut in half.

VARIATION

Crispy Vegetable Rolls
Prepare julienned carrots, beets, and cucumber.
Add these veggies to the wrapper.

Create *3* Variations

"   "
_____

_____

_____

_____

"   "
_____

_____

_____

_____

"   "
_____

_____

_____

_____

_____

The Intuitive Cook's
Asian Tips

• **Sambal Oelek:** A hot, spicy Indonesian and Malaysian condiment. Ingredients: chilies, brown sugar, and salt. I like the Dutch version which I use liberally as a spicy topping for rice and potatoes.

• **Kaffir Lime Leaves:** Essential in Thai cooking. Actually, two leaves joined end to end that have a flora-citrus aroma. Fresh leaves taste much better than dried.

• **Mirin:** Means "rice wine." A low-alcohol, golden wine made from rice. Adds sweetness to Japanese dishes. Used in place of sugar or honey—corn syrup is the main ingredient in Kikkoman's mirin.

• **Oyster sauce:** A rick, thick dark brown sauce made of oysters, brine, and soy sauce. Popular in a variety of Asian dishes.

• **Hoisin sauce:** A sweet and spicy reddish-brown soy bean paste made of garlic, vinegar, chili peppers, sugar, and spices. Mainly a table condiment. Keeps indefinitely if refrigerated. Used in Chinese cooking.

• **Fish sauce:** Made of anchovy extract, salt, and cane sugar. (There is a vegetarian variety.) Use it as you would soy sauce, as a condiment and seasoning. *Caesar Salad Dressing:* Whisk fish sauce with lemon juice, garlic, pepper, and olive oil. Toss with romaine lettuce and parmesan cheese.

-5-

Mexican Formulas

Dave picks tomatoes for Salsa Cruda.

Mexican food has become one the most
popular cuisines in the world.

—DIANA KENNEDY
From My Mexican Kitchen

I grew up in California's San Joaquin Valley. My high school was located in the small town of Sanger, south of Fresno. Half of the student body was Chicano. In my sophomore year, I was one of six pom-pom girls, along with Agnes Hurtado and Carmelita Mendoza.

In the late sixties, my mother, her husband Bill, and Mia, their six-year-old daughter, moved to San Carlos, Sonora, Mexico. They built an oceanfront house, a block from the Shangrila Trailer Court. (Snowbirds flocked there each winter.) For ten years, the trio enjoyed Mexican weather, music, fishing, and handmade tortillas. Today my brother, Eric, his Mexican wife, Catalina, and my niece, Erica, live in San Carlos and own Snowbird Realty.

In the mid-eighties, Dave and I got married in Mexico at the Las Hadas Resort in Manzanillo Bay. We sailed there on our boat. With all of these connections to Mexico, it's no wonder I am attracted to its people and its food.

Salsa Cruda

FORMULA
tomatoes, *chopped*
lemon/lime
onion
garlic
red/green hot pepper
cilantro
salt

Salsa Cruda means "uncooked salsa." Fresh salsas can be kept in the refrigerator for up to five days. Salsa Verde is green salsa, made with tomatillos, cilantro, and green chilies. Frozen salsa is a poor substitute for fresh. Combine the ingredients in a bowl. *No hay problema.*

VARIATIONS
Claudia's Salsa
To fresh tomatoes, Claudia adds a bunch of cilantro, serrano chilis, white onions, lime juice, sea salt, and a little olive oil.

Corn-Off-the-Cob Salsa
Add fresh corn kernels to the basic formula.
Add as much corn as you like.

Papaya Salsa
Add a whole papaya, chopped, without seeds, to the ingredients above.

Create 3 Variations

"   "
_____

_____
_____
_____

"   "
_____

_____
_____
_____

"   "
_____

_____
_____
_____
_____

Mexican Enchiladas

FORMULA
**corn/flour tortillas
red/green canned sauce
fillings
cheese or yogurt
cilantro,** *garnish*

- Cover the bottom of a rectangular baking dish with enchilada sauce.
- Fill the tortillas with one of the fillings below.
- Pour lots of sauce over the enchiladas and sprinkle them with cheese.
- Bake until hot and bubbly. Let set a little before serving.

FILLINGS

Beans-and-Rice Filling
Combine the rice with a small can of chopped/sliced olives. Add scallions, if you wish. Add a can of whole beans to a can of *refritos* (refrieds).
Use the red enchilada sauce.

Tofu-Olive Filling
Combine mashed tofu with green olives, the kinds with pimentos. Add green onion slices, and some grated cheese. Use the green enchilada sauce.

Create *3* Variations

"   "
_____

_____

_____

_____

"   "
_____

_____

_____

_____

"   "
_____

_____

_____

_____

_____

Tantalizing Tacos

FORMULA

flour/corn tortillas
lettuce
olives
avocado
salsa
cheese or yogurt, *topping*
cilantro, *garnish*

Tacos are so easy to make. That's why we all make them frequently and don't need instructions. Tacos lend to simple buffet dinner for big crowds. Kids love them.

FILLINGS

Beans-and-Rice Tacos
First, fill a tortilla with beans and rice, then add
the formula's other ingredients.

Health-Nut Tacos
To amp up the nutitional value of an ordinary taco,
add braised tofu or tempeh strips, grated carrots,
grated beets, spinach or kale leaves,
and alfalfa sprouts.

Create 3 Variations

"   "
_____

_____

_____

_____

"   "
_____

_____

_____

_____

"   "
_____

_____

_____

_____

The Intuitive Cook's
Mexican Tips

• **Get to Know "Quinoa":** A tiny, bead-shaped, cream-colored grain that was popular with the ancient Incas. Quinoa contains more protein and fewer carbs than any other grain, and it has eight amino acids. Quinoa cooks much faster than rice.

• **Go for Glass Containers:** Replace all of your plastic containers with small, medium, and large blue-lidded glass bowls by Pyrex. Also get at least two sets of Working Glasses (Walmart). Snug- fitting white lids for the glasses can be purchased from *thekitchenstore.com* and 800-458-2616. Six lids cost about $1.50. Keep leftovers in glass.

• **Freeze Grains:** I freeze rice and quinoa in small glass Pyrex bowls (see tip above). These grains become fluffy when microwaved or cooked in a skillet.

• **Queso Fresco:** A fresh Mexican cheese that is white and salty. Also called "queso blanco."

• **Mexican Chocolate:** It's called Ibarra and most supermarkets carry it. It's great for hot chocolate and *mole poblano* sauces. Ingredients: cocoa, cinnamon, vanilla, and almonds.

Italian Formulas

A restaurant in the Dolomite mountains,
a long way to hike for a pizza.

*When you blend the golds of Italy—olive oil,
garlic, and Italian herbs and spices—you create
a fragrance for the gods.*

—MARGUERITE DIMONO BUONOPANE
The North End Cookbook

Basil pesto is Italy's greatest contribution to my culinary life. I spread it on freshly-baked bread, stir it into garden vegetable soups, and plop it on steamy baked potatoes. I freeze it for company and give it as a special gift. Dave grows basil year round. I am truly blessed.

In the late nineties, we hiked up and down the Dolomite mountains of Northern Italy, along the romantic shores of Lake Como, and across the steep coastline of the Cinque Terre region.

On the coast, we based out of Vernazza in a quaint little cottage with a basil garden the size of a two-car garage. Its owner, Ursai Aurelio, made pesto in a large marble mortar. It was the best I've ever eaten. Today, I make pesto the quick and easy way, in a food processor. And I reminisce about our Italian experience.

Creamy Risottos

FORMULA
Arborio rice
butter/olive oil
onion, *finely chopped*
garlic, *optional*
white wine, *optional*
stock/water (*keep it hot*)
salt & white pepper
grated cheese, *such as Parmesan, Pecorino, Mozzarella, and Gorgonzola*

Sauté some onion until it is soft. Add rice and cook 2-3 minutes, stirring constantly. Coat the grains well. Next, gradually add white wine and stir until it is absorbed. Then add *hot* stock/water, a ladleful at a time, stirring constantly until absorbed. Mix in the cheese.

VARIATIONS

Wild Mushroom Risotto
Soak the mushrooms (Shantrelles, Porcini, Portabella) until soft. Strain and reserve the water for the risotto. Cook mushrooms in butter and garlic.

Basil & Parsley Risotto
At the end, stir in finely chopped basil and parsley.

Orange Risotto
Add chunks of an orange-fleshed squash and a dash of nutmeg or cinnamon.

Create *3* Variations

"   "
———————————————————————————————

———————————————————————————————

———————————————————————————————

———————————————————————————————

"   "
———————————————————————————————

———————————————————————————————

———————————————————————————————

———————————————————————————————

"   "
———————————————————————————————

———————————————————————————————

———————————————————————————————

———————————————————————————————

———————————————————————————————

Golden Polentas

FORMULA
cornmeal, *coarse ground*
salted water
cheese and/or butter

ADDITIONS
corn kernels
sun-dried tomato bits
hot pepper flakes, *crushed*
kidney or black beans

Cook one part polenta to roughly four parts water. Add more water if necessary. First, bring water to a boil. Then add polenta in a slow steady stream. Cook at medium heat. Stir often. The polenta is done when it pulls away easily from the sides of the pan. Tune into your intuition.

TOPPINGS

Mushroom Topping
Sauté onions and mushrooms in olive oil
and butter. Try a medley of wild mushrooms.
Add finely chopped garlic and parsley.

Store-Bought Toppings
Any bottled pasta sauce can be ladled onto a square
or wedge of polenta. Pestos and tapenades
work well, too.

Create *3* Variations

"   "
_____

_____
_____
_____

"   "
_____

_____
_____
_____

"   "
_____

_____
_____
_____
_____

Crispy Bruschettas

FORMULA
bread, *slices*
garlic, *sliced in half*
olive oil, *extra-virgin*
toppings, *many possibilities*

Toast some sturdy peasant bread slices in your oven until golden brown, dried out, and very crisp. (Don't use a toaster.) Rub one side with garlic and then drizzle with a fruity olive oil.

TOPPINGS

Tomato & Basil Topping
Slice vine-ripened tomatoes in half. Sprinkle them with salt and set them upside down, for about 30 minutes, to drain. Chop the tomatoes. Next combine them with chopped fresh basil leaves. Add freshly ground pepper and a splash of olive oil. Toss gently.

Mushroom Topping
Heat olive oil and butter in a skillet over medium heat. Add mushrooms (one or more types) and garlic. Sauté, stirring frequently. Add finely chopped parsley, salt, and pepper. Cook for a few more minutes.

Create 3 Toppings

"   "
_____

_____
_____
_____

"   "
_____

_____
_____
_____

"   "
_____

_____
_____
_____
_____

Basil Pesto

FORMULA
fresh basil leaves
garlic
walnuts or pine nuts
olive oil
salt
Parmesan cheese

Finely chop the first five ingredients in a food processor. Place in a bowl and then stir in cheese by hand. Pesto is Italian for "pounded." Traditionally, pesto was made by crushing it with a mortar and pestle.

VARIATIONS

Sun-dried Tomato Pesto
Add a dollop of sundried tomatoes to the formula. Another time, add hot sauce and some pinches of dried oregano.

Olive Pesto
A dollop of black olives adds zing to basil pesto.

Macadamia Nut Pesto
Substitute mac-nuts for the pinenuts or walnuts and add a Hawaiian touch. Hang loose.

Create *3* Variations

"   "
_____

_____
_____
_____

"   "
_____

_____
_____
_____

"   "
_____

_____
_____
_____
_____

Lucinda's Pasta Medley

FORMULA
pasta spirals or shells (*not vermicelli***)**
polenta cubes
pinenuts, *toasted*
cheese, *grated*
vegetable(s)
fresh basil
fresh parsley
Italian seasoning mix
pepper flakes or a hot sauce

Cook the pasta. Saute the polenta in garlic and olive oil. Toast the pinenuts. Cook the vegetable. Combine everything in a skillet. Add the cheese and herbs. Enjoy.

VARIATIONS
Broccoli Pasta Medley
Add cooked broccoli to the ingredients above.
This is Lucinda's favorite vegetable for this entrée.

Spinach Pasta Medley
Spinach (chard and kale, too) enhance this entrée.
Steam, drain, and cut up fresh greens. Combine.

Tomato Pasta Medley
Fresh, roasted, or sun-dried tomatoes make
a fabulous addition to any other topping. I prefer
the slow-roasted kind.

Create 3 Variations

"_____"
_____

_____

_____

_____

"_____"
_____

_____

_____

_____

"_____"
_____

_____

_____

_____

_____

The Intuitive Cook's
Italian Tips

• **Parmigiano-Reggiano:** Made from cows raised in Northern Italy and aged 14 months to 4 years. Has a more granular texture and sharper taste than regular parmesan, and costs more. If possible, ask for it from a wheel and grate it at the last minute. Chalk-white spots means it's too dry. Never freeze it. A real delicacy.

• **Fresh Mozzarella:** It's packed in water. Seek the 100-percent buffalo milk variety called *Mozzarella di Bufala*, the best you can buy. Part-skim milk mozzarella is lower in fat than most cheeses.

• **Italian Flat-Leaf Parsley:** Tastes stronger than curly-leaf parsley. Harder to find in supermarkets. A good source of vitamins C and A.

• **Facts about Pasta:** In Italian, pasta means "paste," which describes its dough. Look for pasta made with semolina flour,. This flour absorbs much less water than other flours. Archeologists claim that pasta noodles existed in 1000 B.C.

• ***Pinons:*** Italian for "pine nuts." Pinons are high in fat and become rancid quickly. Store them in your freezer. Toast them in a skillet.

-7-

Middle Eastern Formulas

The early origins of Middle Eastern food can be found in Bedouin dishes and the peasant dishes of each country.

—CLAUDIA RODEN
The New Book of Middle Eastern Food

Garlicky hummus is my favorite Middle Eastern dish. I frequently bring it to potluck dinners and serve it as an appetizer. My signature hummus has a green tint because I add a generous handful of fresh parsley from our garden. I use a lemon from the tree near our chicken coop.

Falafels rank high on my list of the world's most delectable lunch snacks. I tuck falafel balls into pita bread with salad ingredients and then add a dollop of yogurty dressing. The best ones are in Paris in the Jewish district on the Rue de Rosiers.

The Middle East fascinates me because our neighbors are Persians from Iran. Every Friday night, they invite about twenty people for a potluck dinner and belly dancing. Their love of entertaining intrigues me, perhaps because I'm fifty-percent Scandinavian and a more private person.

Classic Hummus

FORMULA

garbanzo beans
garlic
raw tahini
cayenne
cumin seeds, *toasted & ground*
lemon
olive oil
scallions, *optional*
salt & pepper

Place the ingredients in a food processor bowl. Process until smooth. Add a little water if the hummus is too thick. Eat hummus as a dip, rolled up in a tortilla, and spread on pita bread. Garnish with a few garbanzo beans, a sprig of parsley, and a drizzle of olive oil, and freshly ground black pepper.

VARIATIONS

Eggplant Hummus
Add roasted eggplant. If you leave out the garbanzos and add parsley, you'll have an eggplant dip.

Red Pepper Hummus
Add a dollop of roasted red peppers.

Parsley Hummus
Add a handful of finely chopped parsley. Wow!

Create 3 Variations

"   "
_____

_____

_____

_____

"   "
_____

_____

_____

_____

"   "
_____

_____

_____

_____

_____

Pita Pocket Concoctions

FORMULA
pita bread
lettuce
cucumber, seeded and sliced
tomatoes
olives
falafel balls or patties
yogurt or tahini-based sauce
(or a white bottled salad dressing)

- In Syria, Lebanon, and Jordan, falafels are made with a mix of garbanzo and fava beans. In Israel, fava beans are used alone. In Egypt, fava beans are preferred.
- To improve the flavor of a falafel mix, add chopped parsley, scallions and crushed garlic. I don't deep-fry falafels. Instead, I shape them into patties and fry them in small amount of oil.

FILLINGS

Add More Veggies
You can a variety of vegetables to your pita pocket.
Try alfalfa sprouts, grated carrots, artichokes.

Steamed Greens
Steam handfuls of kale, chard, and spinach.
Chopped broccoli and green beans can be added to the greens. Drain well. Top with cheese and cover the pan to melt it. Sprinkle with hot sauce. Finally, slide
the greens into a pita.

Create *3* Variations

"   "
_____

_____

_____

_____

"   "
_____

_____

_____

_____

"   "
_____

_____

_____

_____

_____

Bulgur Wheat Pilaf

FORMULA
bulgur wheat, *or rice, millet, quinoa*
oil/butter
onion
garlic
stock/water

Bulgur wheat is steamed, dried, and then crushed wheat kernels with a chewy texture. Fine, medium, and coarse grinds are available. To make a pilaf, brown a grain in oil or butter and then cook it in stock or water.

VARIATIONS

Raisin & Pine Nut Pilaf
Toss raisins, black or golden, and toasted
pine nuts, into the cooked grain.

Vegetable Pilaf
Toss in a variety of vegetables.

Vermicelli Pilaf
Cut up pieces of a thin spaghetti and add them
to the bulgur just before frying in butter.

Create *3* Variations

"   "
_____

_____

_____

_____

"   "
_____

_____

_____

_____

"   "
_____

_____

_____

_____

Tabouli Salads

FORMULA
bulgur wheat/brown rice/quinoa
parsley, *finely chopped*
(preferably flat-leaf parsley)
mint *(less than parsley)*
scallions
tomatoes, *diced*
lemon/lime juice
olive oil
salt

ADDITIONS
cucumber, *seeded & diced*
garlic, *minced*
pepper
garbanzo beans/lentils
bell pepper
allspice/cinnamon, *just a pinch*

- Wash the bulgur several times. Soak it in water until it is soft, about two hours. Drain it well in a mesh strainer. Press with back of a large spoon to remove even more water.
- Finely chop the vegetables and herbs.
- Combine all ingredients.
- To blend the flavors, refrigerate the tabouli for at least two hours.

Create 3 Variations

"   "
_____

_____

_____

_____

"   "
_____

_____

_____

_____

"   "
_____

_____

_____

_____

_____

The Intuitive Cook's
Middle Eastern Tips

• **Social Customs:** In *The New Book of Middle Eastern Food*, author Claudia Roden says:

(1) Hospitality is a strict duty all over the Middle East. If a guest arrives unexpectedly, the host must never ask why he has come. Mantra: "Give the guest food to eat even if you're starving."

(2) Middle Eastern women are constantly coaxed to perfect family recipes. Cooking ability is rated high among female accomplishments.

(3) To persuade a friend to stay for lunch is a triumph and precious honor. To entertain many is to honor them all mutually.

(4) Middle Easterners turn to food to mark important events—birthdays, weddings, graduations, promotions, and new camels.

(5) Cooking is often done in the company of relatives and friends. You'll see lots of women chopping, stirring, and gossiping in the kitchen.

(6) A legacy of tribal custom says that hospitality is the first requirement for survival.

• **Papaya, Banana and Drizzle of Tahini.** Fill a papaya-half with banana slices and tahini, a nut butter made from ground sesame seeds. Buy raw tahini.

• **A Dessert Mystery:** To confound your dinner guests, layer lemon yogurt and vanilla ice cream in dish.

~&~

The Intuitive Cook's Notebook

To Make the Intuitive Cook's
Notebook

The format of the recipes in *Intuitive Cuisine* may be used in a notebook for cookbook recipes you want to rewrite and save. Just follow these simple steps:

Step 1
Buy a three-ring binder, a set of page-dividers, and package of sheet protectors.

Step 2
Label each divider after the subjects in the table of contents, or make up your own categories.

Step 3
On a copy machine, make heaps of copies of the two-page spreads on pages 110-111 and a few for 112-113. Place the spreads back-to-back in sheet protectors in the subjects of your notebook.

Step 4
When you discover a delicious new recipe, copy its basic FORMULA and your intuitive VARIATIONS onto a format-sheet. Then slip it into a sheet-protector. When you prepare a dish, remove its recipe from the binder and use it in the kitchen.

"_____"

FORMULA:

_____
_____
_____
_____
_____
_____
_____
_____
_____
_____
_____
_____
_____

TO MAKE IT:

(1)

(2)

(3)

(4)

Create 4 Variations

" _____ "
_____

_____
_____
_____

" _____ "
_____

_____
_____
_____

" _____ "
_____

_____
_____
_____

" _____ "
_____

_____
_____
_____

Create *MORE* Variations

"_____"
_____

_____
_____
_____

"_____"
_____

_____
_____
_____

"_____"
_____

_____
_____
_____

"_____"
_____

_____
_____
_____

"_____"

_____

_____

_____

"_____"

_____

_____

_____

"_____"

_____

_____

_____

"_____"

_____

_____

_____

_____

NOTES

NOTES

NOTES

NOTES

For Copies of This Book

Send $12
to the address below:

Egghead Books
Box 223157,
Princeville, HI 96722.

(Ask about our generous quantity discounts.)

The Author

Cris Evatt started writing after holding down a variety jobs, including blackjack dealer, dental hygienist, and graphic designer. She describes herself as a typical Leo, a leader and speaker who delights in sharing her personal epiphanies with others. She writes about relationships, living simply and getting organized. "Simplicity doesn't happen by chance," says Cris. "You must have a drive, an urge, to make things simpler." She edits her possessions often, tossing out things she no longer loves or uses. Besides cooking, her passions include yoga, hiking, swimming, traveling, and reading in cozy cafés. She lives in Hawaii with her laid-back husband, Dave, and their irascible cat, Fern.